United States Government Accountability Office

Report to the Ranking Member, Committee on Homeland Security and Governmental Affairs, United States Senate

July 2014

I0410352

SPACE LAUNCH SYSTEM

Resources Need to be Matched to Requirements to Decrease Risk and Support Long Term Affordability

GAO-14-631

July 2014

GAO Highlights

Highlights of GAO-14-631, a report to the Ranking Member, Committee on Homeland Security and Governmental Affairs U.S. Senate

SPACE LAUNCH SYSTEM

Resources Need to be Matched to Requirements to Decrease Risk and Support Long Term Affordability

Why GAO Did This Study

SLS is NASA's first exploration-class heavy lift launch vehicle in over 40 years. Predecessor programs, such as Constellation, were canceled in the face of acquisition problems and funding shortfalls. NASA estimates it could spend almost $12 billion developing the first of three SLS vehicle variants and associated ground systems through initial launch in late 2017 and potentially billions more to develop increasingly capable vehicles. Ensuring that this program is affordable and sustainable for the long term is a key goal of the 2013 National Space Transportation Policy.

GAO was asked to evaluate SLS program challenges. This report examines (1) the SLS program's progress toward and risks for its first test flight in 2017 and (2) the extent to which the SLS program has plans in place to achieve its long-term goals and promote affordability. To do this, GAO reviewed relevant design, development, cost, and schedule documents; interviewed program officials; and evaluated SLS program actions using acquisition and cost estimating best practices.

What GAO Recommends

Among other actions to reduce risk and allow for continued assessment of SLS progress and affordability, GAO recommends that NASA develop an executable business case for SLS that matches resources to requirements, and provide to the Congress an assessment of the SLS elements that could be competitively procured for future SLS variants before finalizing acquisition plans for those variants. NASA concurred with GAO's recommendations.

View GAO-14-631. For more information, contact Cristina Chaplain at (202) 512-4841 or chaplainc@gao.gov.

What GAO Found

The Space Launch System (SLS) program is making solid progress on the SLS design. However, the National Aeronautics and Space Administration (NASA) has not developed an executable business case based on matching the program's cost and schedule resources with the requirement to develop the vehicle and conduct the first flight test in December 2017 at the required confidence level of 70 percent. NASA uses a calculation referred to as the "joint cost and schedule confidence level" to estimate the probable success of a program meeting its cost and schedule targets. NASA policy usually requires a 70 percent confidence level for a program to proceed with final design and fabrication. GAO's work on best practices has shown that programs that do not establish an executable business case that matches requirements—or customer needs—to resources, such as schedule and funding—are at increased risk of cost and schedule growth. The program is satisfying many of NASA's metrics that measure progress against design goals, such as requirements for design maturity. According to the program's risk analysis, however, the agency's current funding plan for SLS may be $400 million short of what the program needs to launch by 2017. Furthermore, the development schedule of the core stage—which drives the SLS schedule—is compressed to meet the 2017 launch date. NASA also faces challenges integrating existing hardware that was not originally designed to fly on SLS. For example, SLS is using solid rocket boosters from the Constellation program, but integrating a new non-asbestos insulating material into the booster design has proven difficult and required changes to the booster manufacturing processes.

The SLS program has not yet defined specific mission requirements beyond the second flight test in 2021 or defined specific plans for achieving long-term goals, but the program has opportunities to promote affordability moving forward. NASA plans to incrementally develop more capable SLS launch vehicles to satisfy long-term goals, but future missions have not been determined, which will directly affect the program's future development path and flight schedule. Mission selection will likely determine which element the program decides to develop next, as the program can afford to develop only one element at a time. The magnitude of these development efforts could be significant but is currently unknown as the program has not developed complete life-cycle cost estimates for the initial or future SLS launch vehicles. In May 2014, GAO recommended that NASA address this issue, and NASA partially concurred, citing that actions taken to structure the programs and track costs met the intent of the recommendations. However, GAO believes NASA's responses do not fully address the concerns about the program's cost estimates. There are opportunities, however, to improve long-term affordability through competition once the development path has been determined and NASA can finalize its acquisition approach. For example, the program plans to compete the procurement of one element; however, the agency has not finalized assessments of options for competitively procuring other future elements. Such assessments could better position NASA to sustain competition, control costs, and better inform Congress about the long-term affordability of the program. GAO's body of work on contracting has shown that competition in contracting is a key factor in controlling cost.

Contents

Abbreviations

CDR	critical design review
EM-1	Exploration Mission 1
EM-2	Exploration Mission 2
EVM	earned value management
ICPS	Interim Cryogenic Propulsion Stage
JCL	Join Cost and Schedule Confidence Level
KDP	key decision point
MDR	mission definition review
mt	metric ton
NASA	National Aeronautics and Space Administration
NFS	National Aeronautics and Space Administration Federal Acquisition Regulation Supplement
Orion	Orion Multi-Purpose Crew Vehicle
PDR	preliminary design review
SDR	system definition review
SIR	system integration review
SLS	Space Launch System
UCA	undefinitized contract action

GAO U.S. GOVERNMENT ACCOUNTABILITY OFFICE

441 G St. N.W.
Washington, DC 20548

July 23, 2014

The Honorable Tom Coburn, M.D.
Ranking Member
Committee on Homeland Security and Governmental Affairs
United States Senate

Dear Senator Coburn:

The National Aeronautics and Space Administration (NASA) is in the midst of developing its first exploration-class heavy lift launch vehicle in over 40 years—the Space Launch System (SLS). The SLS will expand NASA's exploration capability to include crewed flights beyond Earth's orbit. NASA's attempts over the past two decades to develop a successor to the Space Shuttle have been unsuccessful. Prior development programs, the most recent being the Constellation program, were canceled in the face of acquisition problems and funding-related issues. The nearly $12 billion in funding that NASA estimates it could spend developing SLS and associated ground systems through its first launch in late 2017 represents not only a significant portion of NASA's planned budget for major projects during that period but also a significant portion of governmentwide launch-related research and development funding. Developing an exploration program that will be affordable and sustainable for the long term is a key goal of the 2013 National Space Transportation Policy.[1]

GAO has designated NASA's management of acquisitions as a high-risk area for more than two decades in view of persistent cost growth and schedule slippage in the majority of its major projects.[2] While the agency has made progress in recent years in reducing risk on smaller-scale, less complex projects, demonstrating that this progress can be translated to larger, more complex projects, such as SLS, is important. In light of these issues and the long-term significance of the program, you requested that we review the challenges facing NASA's SLS program. This report examines (1) NASA's progress toward the first SLS test flight in 2017 and

---

[1] The White House, National Space Transportation Policy (Washington, D.C.: Nov. 21, 2013).

[2] GAO, *High-Risk Series: An Update*, GAO-13-283 (Washington, D.C.: February 2013).

any acquisition risks associated with its plans and (2) the extent to which the SLS program has plans in place to achieve its long-term goals and promote affordability.

In order to assess NASA's progress to conduct its first flight in 2017, we interviewed and obtained briefings and relevant documents from NASA and contractor officials. We identified and evaluated technical and programmatic issues associated with each major SLS subsystem, by reviewing development plans and discussing relevant issues with agency officials. We also compared planned to actual progress in maturing system designs. We assessed NASA's risk mitigation plans to gauge progress in addressing technical issues and to evaluate the potential impact to scheduled events such as delivery and flight dates. We also reviewed other technical and programmatic indicators and progress made addressing required actions from programmatic reviews at both the subsystem and vehicle level. We evaluated the program's progress toward the 2017 launch date by comparing actual cost, schedule, and performance to current program baselines. To assess long-term affordability, we discussed long-term development plans in support of future missions with agency officials. For purposes of assessing the cost estimate, we reviewed NASA preliminary cost estimates for the SLS, Orion crew capsule that will launch atop SLS, and associated ground systems programs and information related to the baseline cost estimates to determine the scope of the estimates. We assessed the estimates' scope against best practices criteria outlined in GAO's cost estimating guidebook as well as NASA's own requirements and guidance.[3] Furthermore, we evaluated the program's development and acquisition plans to compete future variants of the SLS by reviewing contract information, including any follow-on contract options, and discussing supplier availability with agency officials. For more information on our scope and methodology, see appendix I.

We conducted this performance audit from June 2013 to July 2014 in accordance with generally accepted government auditing standards.

---

[3] GAO, *GAO Cost Estimating and Assessment Guide: Best Practices for Developing and Managing Capital Program Costs,* GAO-09-3SP (Washington, D.C.: March 2009). The Guide is a compilation of best practices that federal cost estimating organizations and industry use to develop and maintain reliable cost estimates throughout the life of a government acquisition program. NASA Procedural Requirements (NPR) 7120.5E, *NASA Space Flight Program and Project Management Requirements,* § 2.4 (Aug. 14, 2012); and NASA, *2008 NASA Cost Estimating Handbook* (Washington, D.C.).

Those standards require that we plan and perform the audit to obtain sufficient, appropriate evidence to provide a reasonable basis for our findings and conclusions based on our audit objectives. We believe that the evidence obtained provides a reasonable basis for our findings and conclusions based on our audit objectives.

Background

The National Aeronautics and Space Administration Authorization Act of 2010 directed NASA to, among another things, develop a Space Launch System as a follow-on to the Space Shuttle and as a key component in expanding human presence beyond low-Earth orbit. To that end, NASA plans to incrementally develop three progressively more capable SLS launch vehicles—70-, 105-, and 130-metric ton (mt) variants. When complete, the 130-mt vehicle is expected to have more launch capability than the Saturn V vehicle, which was used for Apollo missions, and be significantly more capable than any recent or current launch vehicle. The act also directed NASA to prioritize the core elements with the goal of operational capability for the core elements not later than December 2016.[4] NASA subsequently negotiated an extension of that date, to December 2017, based on the agency's assessment of the tasks associated with developing the new launch vehicle.

In 2011, NASA formally established the SLS program. To fulfill the direction of the 2010 act, the agency plans to develop the three SLS launch vehicle capabilities, complemented by the Orion Multi-Purpose Crew Vehicle (Orion) to transport humans and cargo into space. The first version of the SLS that NASA is developing is a 70-mt launch vehicle known as Block I. NASA expects to conduct two test flights of the Block I vehicle—the first in 2017 and the second in 2021. The vehicle is scheduled to fly an uncrewed Orion some 70,000 kilometers beyond the moon during the first test flight, known as Exploration Mission-1 (EM-1), and to fly a second mission known as Exploration Mission-2 (EM-2) beyond the moon to further test performance with a crewed Orion vehicle. After 2021, NASA intends to build 105- and 130-mt launch vehicles, known respectively as Block IA/B and Block II, which it expects to use as the backbone of manned spaceflight for decades.[5] The agency plans for

---

[4] Pub. L. No. 111-267, §§ 302(c)(2), 303(a)(2) (codified at 42 U.S.C. §§ 18322, 18323).

[5] NASA plans for SLS Block IA to utilize advanced boosters, Block IB an exploration upper stage, and Block II the advanced boosters and exploration upper stage. The agency has not yet determined whether it will first develop the Block IA or Block IB variant.

these vehicles to carry larger cargo and travel farther into space, but it has not yet selected specific missions for the increased capabilities to be provided by Block IA/B and Block II. NASA anticipates using the Block IA/B vehicles for destinations such as near-Earth asteroids and LaGrange points and the Block II vehicles for eventual Mars missions.[6]

NASA's Acquisition Life Cycle

NASA plans to evolve the 70-mt SLS design following the agency's life cycle acquisition process for flight systems. That process is defined by two broad phases—formulation and implementation—and several key decision points.[7] These broad phases are then further divided into more discrete pieces with different purposes: pre-phase A through phase F. See figure 1 for a depiction of NASA's life cycle for flight systems.

---

[6] In a two-body system, such as Earth and the sun, there are points nearby where a third object can be positioned and remain in place relative to the other two objects. These are known as Lagrange points.

[7] NASA defines the formulation phase as the identification of how the program or project supports the agency's strategic goals; the assessment of feasibility, technology, concepts, and performance of trade studies; risk assessment and possible risk mitigations and continuous risk management processes; team building, development of operations concepts and acquisition strategies; establishment of high-level requirements, requirements flow down, and success criteria; assessing the relevant industrial base/supply chain to ensure program or project success, the preparation of plans, cost estimates, budgets, and schedules essential to the success of a program or project; and the establishment of control systems to ensure performance of those plans and alignment with current agency strategies. NPR 7120.5E, § 1.3.1.a (Aug. 14, 2012). The implementation phase is defined as the execution of approved plans for the development and operation of the program or project, and the use of control systems to ensure performance to approved plans and requirements and continued alignment with the agency's strategic goals. NPR 7120.5E, §1.3.1.c (Aug. 14, 2012).

Figure 1: NASA's Life Cycle for Flight Systems

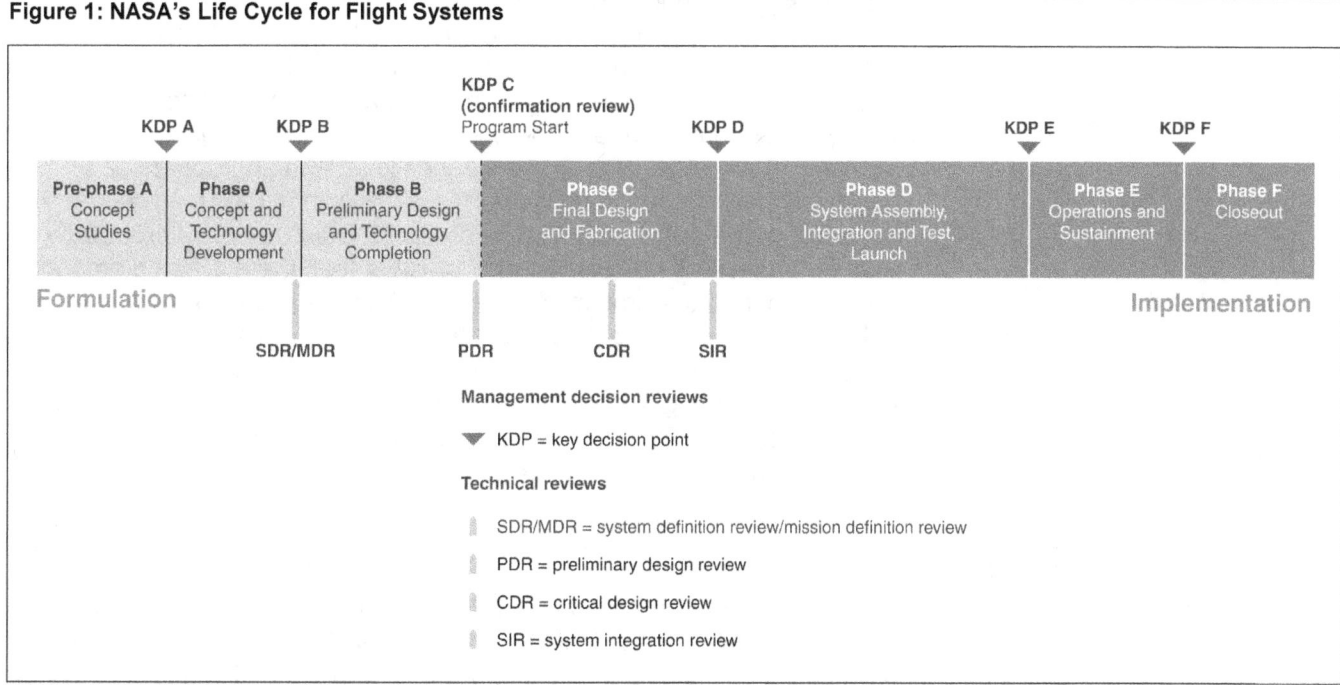

Source: NASA data and GAO analysis. | GAO-14-631

During formulation, programs develop and define requirements and establish cost and schedule baselines and an acquisition strategy. Formulation concludes with a preliminary design review (PDR) and project confirmation review where cost and schedule baselines are confirmed and documented in the agency baseline commitment.[8] The PDR evaluates the completeness and consistency of the planning, technical, and cost and schedule baselines developed during formulation. It assesses compliance of the preliminary design with applicable requirements, and determines if the project is sufficiently mature to begin the final design and fabrication phase. The agency baseline commitment establishes and documents an integrated set of requirements, cost, schedule, technical content, and an agreed-to joint cost and schedule confidence level (JCL) that forms the basis for NASA's commitment with

---

[8] NPR 7120.5E, (Aug. 14, 2012).

the Office of Management and Budget and the Congress.[9] These baselines are informed by the JCL process. The JCL is a probabilistic analysis that provides assurance to stakeholders that programs will meet cost and schedule targets. In general, programs' cost and schedule baselines are based on a 70 percent confidence level, unless the decision authority approves a different confidence level with appropriate justification and documentation.[10] This is the point on the joint cost and schedule probability distribution where there is a 70 percent probability that the project will be completed at or lower than the estimated amount and at or before the projected schedule. Program progress can subsequently be measured against the baseline commitments.[11] NASA's policy requires that a JCL be developed at a program's confirmation review.[12] According to agency officials, NASA is currently establishing the JCL for SLS and the program will move into the implementation phase when the confirmation review is complete.

Acquisition Best Practices

GAO's best practices for systems acquisition state that evolutionary acquisition is a commercial best practice.[13] In evolutionary acquisition, a program uses mature technologies and capabilities that fit within existing resources to field initial capabilities sooner and gradually develops progressively more capable increments until it achieves its ultimate requirements. This approach is considered a best practice because it allows commercial companies and the government to develop and produce more sophisticated products faster and less expensively.

GAO's work on best practices has also shown that success in development efforts such as SLS depends on establishing an executable business case based on matching requirements and resources before committing to a new product development effort. In its simplest form, a business case requires a balance between the concept selected to satisfy customer needs and the resources—technologies, design knowledge,

---

[9] NPR 7120.5E, Appendix A (Aug. 14, 2012).

[10] NPR 7120.5E, § 2.4 (Aug. 14, 2012).

[11] NPR 7120.5E, Table 2-5 (Aug. 14, 2012).

[12] NPR 7120.5E, § 2.4 (Aug. 14, 2012).

[13] GAO, *Best Practices: Capturing Design and Manufacturing Knowledge Early Improves Acquisition Outcomes*, GAO-03-645T (Washington, D.C.: Jul. 15, 2002).

GAO-14-631 Space Launch System

funding, time, and management capacity—needed to transform the concept into a product. At the heart of a business case is a knowledge-based approach that requires that managers demonstrate high levels of knowledge as the program proceeds from technology development to system development and, finally, production. Ideally, with such an approach, key technologies are demonstrated before development begins, the design is stabilized before prototypes are built or production begins, and testing is used to validate product maturity at each level. At each decision point, the balance among time, money, and capacity is confirmed. In essence, knowledge supplants risk over time. Having adequate knowledge about requirements and resources is particularly important for a program like SLS because human spaceflight development projects are complex, difficult, and costly.

We have found that within NASA's acquisition framework, the PDR and corresponding confirmation review are the point at which development projects should have a sound business case in hand.[14] NASA's Systems Engineering Policy states that this review demonstrates that the preliminary design meets all system requirements with acceptable risk and within the cost and schedule constraints. After a project is confirmed following PDR, it begins implementation during which time senior NASA officials periodically review the programmatic and technical status of projects and verify the project's readiness to proceed forward. For example, a critical design review (CDR) before the project's subsystems are integrated evaluates the integrity of the project design and its ability to meet mission requirements, with appropriate margins and acceptable risk, within defined project constraints, including available resources. In short, the CDR determines if the design is appropriately mature to support proceeding with the final design and fabrication phase.[15] Our past work on product development best practices has found that programs having at least 90 percent of engineering drawings releasable by the critical design review lower their risk of subsequent cost growth and schedule delays, and guidance in NASA's *Systems Engineering Handbook* mirrors this

---

[14] GAO, *NASA: Implementing a Knowledge-Based Acquisition Framework Could Lead to Better Investment Decisions and Project Outcomes*, GAO-06-218 (Washington, D.C.: Dec. 21, 2005), and *NASA: Agency Has Taken Steps Toward Making Sound Investment Decisions for Ares I but Still Faces Challenging Knowledge Gaps*, GAO-08-51 (Washington, D.C.: Oct. 31, 2007).

[15] NPR 7120.5E, Table 2-5 (Aug. 14, 2012).

metric.[16] NASA also tracks both mass margin and resolution of requests for action, which are technical, safety, and programmatic comments from independent reviewers, as additional measures of design maturity.[17] In addition, experts in the space community have identified other metrics that can be useful to assess the design stability of unique space systems.[18] These include the program's level of funding reserves and schedule margin at various points in the development life cycle as well as the percent of verification and validation plans completed at both PDR and CDR.

Elements of SLS

In accordance with direction contained in the NASA Authorization Act of 2010, NASA's acquisition approach for building the initial variant of the SLS is predicated on the use of legacy systems, designs, and contracts from the Space Shuttle and Constellation programs. Figure 2 provides details about the heritage of each SLS hardware element and its source.

---

[16] GAO, GAO-03-645T; GAO-06-218; *Best Practices: Using a Knowledge-based Approach to Improve Weapon Acquisition*, GAO-04-386SP (Washington, D.C.: Jan. 1, 2004); and NASA, *Systems Engineering Handbook*, NASA/SP-2007-6105 Rev1 (Washington, D.C.: December 2007).

[17] Mass is a measurement of how much matter is in an object. It is related to an object's weight, which is mathematically equal to mass multiplied by acceleration due to gravity. Margin is the spare amount of mass or power allowed or given for contingencies or special situations.

[18] GAO, *NASA: Assessments of Selected Large-Scale Projects*, GAO-14-338SP (Washington, D.C.: Apr. 15, 2014).

Figure 2: SLS and Orion Hardware Elements

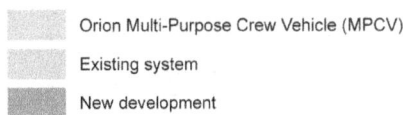

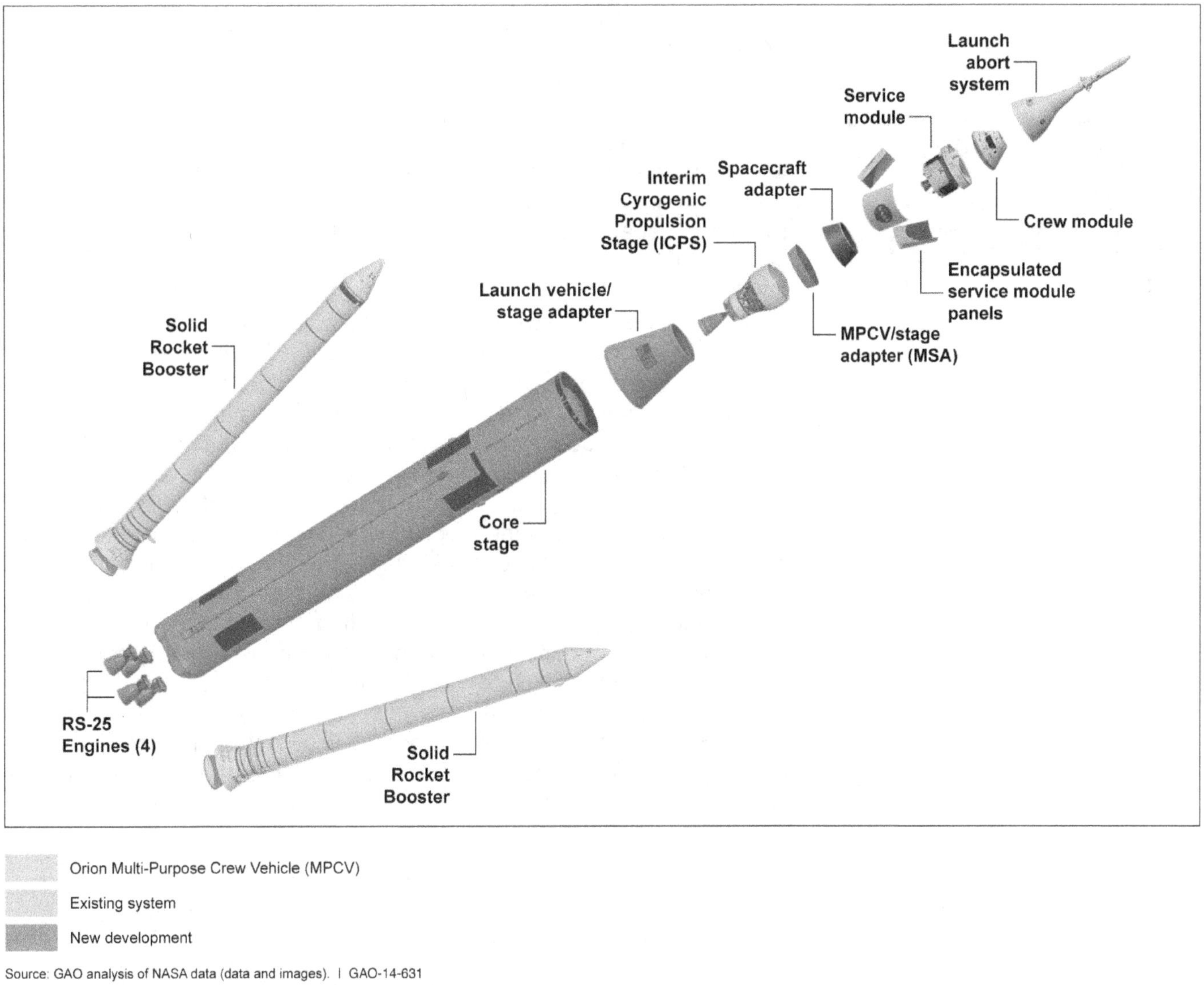

Orion Multi-Purpose Crew Vehicle (MPCV)

Existing system

New development

Source: GAO analysis of NASA data (data and images). | GAO-14-631

NASA plans to use 16 RS-25 engines remaining from the Space Shuttle program to provide power for up to four flights of the SLS. Similarly, the agency is procuring five-segment boosters that were developed under the Constellation program to provide thrust during the initial minutes of SLS flight. NASA is also procuring a cryogenic rocket stage used on United Launch Alliance's Delta IV launch vehicle and modifying it to operate as the Interim Cryogenic Propulsion Stage (ICPS) to provide in-space power for SLS. Finally, the design for the new core stage, which functions as the SLS's fuel tank and structural backbone, is derived from the Shuttle's external tank and Ares I upper stage.

Program's Ability to Meet Schedule for 2017 Test Flight at Risk

While the SLS program is satisfying many of NASA's metrics that measure progress against overall design goals, NASA has not established an executable business case that matches the SLS program's cost and schedule resources with the requirement to develop the SLS and launch the first flight test in December 2017 at the required confidence level of 70 percent.[19] Matching resources to requirements is considered a best practice for establishing a successful acquisition program.[20] Reduced confidence levels increase the risk that the program will miss its launch date or overrun its cost baseline. The program is on target to achieve goals for design drawing release and mass and expects to meet necessary documentation requirements for its critical design review. However, the development schedule of the core stage, which is driving the overall program schedule, is aggressive and substantial amounts of schedule that the program reserved to resolve unanticipated issues is already threatened. NASA has focused on integration issues, and the program is on plan for closing design trades, environmental studies, and design interface documents that are intended to reduce this risk. However, the modification and integration of heritage elements may be a challenge—one which NASA often underestimates. In addition, according to the program's risk analysis, the agency's current funding plan for SLS may be $400 million short of what the program needs to launch by 2017. This funding discrepancy was, in part, responsible for the significant delay in finalizing the contracts for element development,

---

[19] NASA's procedural requirements require Mission Directorates to plan and budget programs and projects with an estimated life-cycle cost greater than $250 million based on a 70 percent Joint Cost and Schedule Confidence Level (JCL), or at a different level as approved by the Decision Authority, which for SLS is the NASA Associate Administrator. Any JCL approved by the Decision Authority at less than 70 percent must be justified and documented. The JCL is a quantitative probability analysis that requires the project to combine its cost, schedule, and risks into a complete quantitative picture to help assess whether the project will be successfully completed within cost and on schedule. NPR 7120.5E, §§2.4.4, 2.4.4.1, 2.4.3.2 (Aug. 14, 2012).

[20] GAO, GAO-04-386SP and *Best Practices: Better Matching of Needs and Resources Will lead to Better Weapon System Outcomes*, GAO-01-288 (Washington, D.C.: Mar. 8, 2001).

which increased cost and schedule risk to the government as well as reduced visibility into contractor performance.

NASA Has Not Matched Resources and Requirements for 2017 Initial Flight Test

NASA has not established an executable business case based on matching the SLS program's cost and schedule resources with the requirement to develop the SLS and launch the first flight test in December 2017 at the required confidence level of 70 percent. NASA delayed the SLS key decision point C decision from October 2013 to at least July 2014, as the agency considered future plans for the program. If the agency determines the current funding plan for SLS is insufficient to match requirements to resources for the December 2017 flight test at the 70 percent confidence level, the agency's options for matching resources to requirements are largely limited to increasing program funding, delaying the schedule or accepting a reduced confidence level for the initial flight test. While the program's decision authority is allowed in some instances to approve a confidence level of less than 70 percent, doing so increases the likelihood that the program will miss the launch date or overrun the current cost estimate. Should cost growth or schedule delay occur, it could place other programs' funding at risk if NASA chooses to take planned funding from those programs in order to maintain the SLS schedule. Although cost and schedule growth can occur on any project, increases associated with NASA's most costly and complex missions—such as SLS, which makes up about 9 percent of NASA's annual budget—can have dramatic effects on the availability of funding for NASA's portfolio of major projects.

Funding levels have impaired the SLS program's ability to match requirements to resources since its inception. As illustrated in figure 3, NASA has requested relatively consistent amounts of funding for SLS each year. According to agency officials, the program has taken steps to live within that flat funding profile, including streamlining program office operations and asking each contractor to identify efficiencies in their production processes. Even so, according to the program's own analysis, going into the confirmation review, SLS's top risk was that the current planned budget through 2017 would be insufficient to allow the SLS as designed to meet the EM-1 flight date. The SLS program office calculated the risk associated with insufficient funding through 2017 as having a 90 percent likelihood of occurrence; furthermore, it indicated the insufficient budget could push the planned December 2017 launch date out 6 months and add some $400 million to the overall cost of SLS development. Program officials stated that the potential cost impacts of this risk were considerably higher in the past, but that they were able to reduce the impact due to receiving more funding than requested in fiscal years 2013 and 2014.

Figure 3: SLS Funding Requested, Fiscal Years 2012-2016

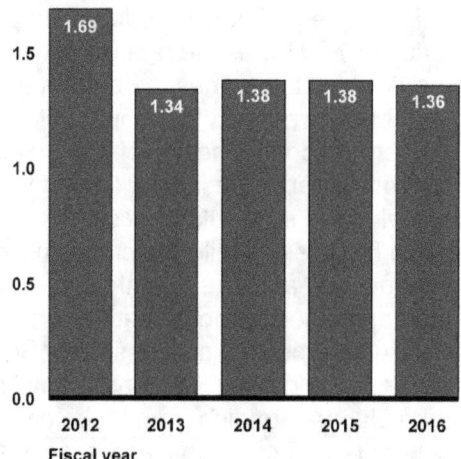

Dollars (in billions)

Source: GAO analysis of NASA budget data. I GAO-14-631

Note: Fiscal year 2016 funding estimate is notional.

In May 2014, the House Committee on Appropriations report—which accompanied the Commerce, Justice, Science, and Related Agencies Appropriations Bill, 2015—"expressed frustration with NASA's practices of requesting arbitrarily reduced funding levels for SLS and insisting that the program manage to an inefficient flat-line budget profile." The Committee noted that this practice has "detrimental results" and is likely to lead to a "launch delay for EM-1 and deferral of long-lead work needed for the timely achievement of EM-2 and other future flights." In light of these and other issues, the Committee has chosen to recommend maintaining SLS vehicle development funding at the fiscal year 2014 enacted level of $1.6 billion.

Best practices for acquisition programs indicate that matching resources to requirements and rationally balancing cost, schedule, and performance is a key step in establishing a successful acquisition program.[21] We have also found that NASA's previous attempts to develop new transportation systems, such as the Constellation program, have failed in part because they were focused on maturing designs without adequate funding to support those efforts.[22] Our work has also shown that developing a sound business case before committing resources to development—which includes firm requirements, mature technologies, a knowledge-based acquisition strategy, a realistic cost estimate, and sufficient funding and time—would help mitigate the risks inherent in NASA's programs.[23]

SLS Program Is Meeting Some Design Goals for 2017 Test Flight but Challenges Could Threaten Launch Date

Design Goals

NASA's metrics indicate that the program is on track to meet many of its design goals for demonstrating the initial capability of SLS. Based on our review of top level design metrics that the program is tracking, the program is currently meeting its plan for design drawing release for the core stage, where most of the new design work is occurring. As of May 2014 the program had released 82 percent of the core stage drawings and expects to have 95 percent released by the core stage CDR in July 2014. The program as a whole expects to release 95 percent of its design

---

[21] GAO-04-386SP and GAO-01-288.

[22] GAO, *Space Transportation: Status of the X-33 Reusable Launch Vehicle Program*, GAO/NSIAD-99-176 (Washington, D.C.: Aug. 11, 1999); *National Aero-Space Plane: Restructuring Future Research and Development Efforts*, GAO/NSIAD-93-71, (Washington, D.C.: Dec. 3, 1992); and *NASA: Constellation Program Cost and Schedule Will Remain Uncertain Until a Sound Business Case Is Established*, GAO-09-844 (Washington, D.C.: Aug. 26, 2009).

[23] GAO, *Defense Acquisitions: Key Decisions to Be Made on Future Combat System*, GAO-07-376 (Washington, D.C.: Mar. 15, 2007); *Defense Acquisitions: Improved Business Case Key for Future Combat System's Success*, GAO-06-564T (Washington, D.C.: Apr. 4, 2006); GAO-06-218; and *NASA's Space Vision: Business Case for Prometheus 1 Needed to Ensure Requirements Match Available Resources*, GAO-05-242 (Washington, D.C.: Feb. 28, 2005).

drawings by the program level CDR in March 2015, which exceeds the best practice metric for design drawing release at CDR.[24] Because the CDR is the time in a project's life cycle when the integrity of the project design and its ability to meet mission requirements are assessed, it is important that a project's design is stable enough to warrant continuation with design and fabrication, which is evidenced by release of 90 percent of design drawings at CDR. A stable design allows projects to "freeze" the design and minimize changes prior to beginning the fabrication of hardware. It also helps to avoid re-engineering and rework efforts due to design changes that can be costly to the project in terms of time and funding.

The program is also meeting or close to meeting several design goals related to SLS mass margin and program documentation. As of May 2014, SLS had sufficient mass margin to meet its design goals for EM-1; however, the program has less mass margin for some EM-2 test flight mission options in 2021. If mass becomes an issue leading into EM-2, the vehicle may require design changes that could lead to cost and schedule growth. While the program is behind on its own schedule for addressing the requests for action from the preliminary design review, the program's current plan indicates that all requests will be addressed prior to the CDR scheduled for 2015. In addition to these overall design goals, the program's verification and validation plan, which aids in assessing whether a chosen development solution is capable of meeting its intended purpose and if the system is being developed according to agency requirements, was baselined and approved at PDR with one exception that the program expects to resolve in 2014. With regards to finalizing interface control documents, which define requirements for how systems will connect and interact with one another, the program is 4 percent behind its planned schedule for determining interface requirements by CDR. According to NASA, these documents should help reduce integration issues, such as those between the heritage hardware elements and new core stage, by specifying interaction between the

---

[24] Engineering drawings are considered to be a good measure of the demonstrated stability of a product's design because the drawings represent the language used by engineers to communicate to the manufacturers the details of a new product design—what it looks like, how its components interface, how it functions, how to build it, and what critical materials and processes are required to fabricate and test it. Once the design of a product is finalized, the drawing is "releasable."

heritage elements and core stage, as well as provide a set of interface definitions for when new elements are being designed.

Aggressive Schedule

Although the program is making progress against its design metrics, the core stage development schedule is aggressive and already threatened, and any delays could impair SLS readiness for first flight in 2017. The core stage development drives the SLS schedule because it represents the critical path of activities that must be completed to maintain the program's schedule as a whole. Based on our review of NASA documentation and discussions with program officials, it is clear that the core stage's major program milestones and developmental activities are tightly spaced. For example, the program is allowing 18 months from the point at which it evaluates the design at PDR in January 2013 to the point at which it expects the design to be fully mature at the core stage CDR in July 2014. By comparison, the Ares I project within the Constellation program planned for about 2 years between PDR and CDR. NASA officials indicated that they compressed the core stage development schedule in order to meet the SLS 2017 launch date. The schedule allows for 7 months of schedule reserve after CDR and before the core stage ships to Kennedy Space Center for integration into the SLS, which NASA believes will allow time to address problems it could encounter during development. While allowing 7 months of schedule reserve generally complies with NASA guidance for space flight projects, it may prove insufficient in this instance because the program has already identified a number of threats to the schedule.[25]

The SLS program is tracking threats to the core stage schedule that could take up as much as 70 percent of the 7 months of reserve. Many of these threats are associated with the schedule for acquiring liquid oxygen feeder lines that provide liquid oxygen from the fuel tanks within the core stage to the core stage engine. Agency officials indicated the program is encountering difficulties acquiring feeder lines from available suppliers to meet the core stage development schedule because the feeder lines are larger and will be used in more stressful environments than the lines that suppliers have manufactured in the past. The feeder lines must still be designed, built, and tested for operation in the SLS environment before they can be delivered for integration into the system. While these challenges are not overly complex from a technical viewpoint, resolving

---

[25] NASA, Goddard Procedural Requirements 7120.7 (May 4, 2008).

such threats to the schedule is critical because the element is in early development phases and still has several significant milestones and developmental activities ahead. For example, the core stage has CDR currently scheduled for July 2014 that will assess the program's design maturity. Further, qualification testing to determine if system components meet requirements is currently scheduled to begin in January 2015. As we have found in the past, the integration and test phase of development is generally where issues that require unexpected time and resources to address are discovered.[26]

Heritage Hardware

The SLS program could experience additional schedule pressure if unanticipated challenges associated with using heritage hardware occur when integrating it into the launch vehicle's operational environment and modifying manufacturing process to incorporate new materials. The use of heritage hardware—legacy engine, booster, and propulsion systems—was prescribed in the NASA Authorization Act of 2010, but the hardware was not originally designed for SLS. Therefore, the SLS program must ensure each heritage hardware element meets SLS performance requirements and current design standards prior to the 2017 test flight. Although the heritage hardware challenges have yet to affect the SLS schedule, each heritage hardware element shares the common issue of operating in the SLS environment that is likely to be more stressful than that of its original launch vehicle as well as unique integration issues particular to that element, which must be resolved prior to SLS first flight in 2017. For example, according to agency officials the engines from the Space Shuttle require additional heat shielding because of the increased temperatures they will experience in the SLS environment, and the avionics within the solid rocket boosters from the Constellation program are likely to require additional cushioning to protect them from increased vibrations. Until the core stage is demonstrated, however, the SLS operating environment can be defined only through analytical predictions. Further, eliminating asbestos as a key insulating material within the solid rocket boosters on the SLS has required changes to the booster manufacturing processes to meet safety requirements.

According to agency officials, the challenges they face are typical of those expected when heritage hardware is integrated into a new system. They

---

[26] GAO, *NASA: Assessments of Selected Large-Scale Projects*, GAO-13-276SP (Washington, D.C.: Apr. 17, 2013).

also noted that addressing these challenges involves less time, money, and overall effort than developing new hardware and that each heritage hardware element has schedule reserves to address anticipated integration challenges as well as unknown issues that might arise. Nevertheless, the engineering effort required to address them is significant and, as found by both GAO's and the NASA Inspector General's prior work, the complexity associated with required modifications and problems with availability of components used on projects is often underestimated.[27]

Unclear Scope and Funding Uncertainties Increased Risk by Delaying Contract Definitization

Uncertainty regarding resources increased risk to the program because contracts were not finalized and complete contractor performance data was not provided. According to agency officials, the program was delayed in definitizing contracts, in part, due to resource uncertainty. As a result, the SLS program contractors have worked for extended periods of time without contract definitization—meaning no final agreement on the terms and conditions of their contracts has been negotiated with the government—which put the government at risk of increased costs and limited the program's ability to monitor contractor progress. Contractors have performed, and are performing, work under undefinitized contract actions (UCA) until their respective contracts are definitized and cost and schedule baselines are set. Contract actions such as these authorize contractors to begin work before reaching a final agreement with the government on contract terms and conditions. The government is thus in a weaker position to control costs.

The NASA supplement to the Federal Acquisition Regulation (NFS) provides that the NASA goal is to definitize UCAs within 180 days of issuance, or approximately 6 months.[28] Officials stated that the agency's ability to definitize the element contracts was impacted by the need to use existing contracts, as directed by the NASA Authorization Act of 2010, and to complete work necessary to define requirements and modify those contracts in order to accommodate the SLS effort's scope and content.

---

[27] GAO, *NASA: Assessments of Selected Large-Scale Projects*, GAO-12-207SP, (Washington, D.C.: Mar. 1, 2012), and NASA Office of Inspector General, *NASA's Challenges to Meeting Cost, Schedule, and Performance Goals*, IG-12-021, (Washington, D.C.: Sept. 27, 2012).

[28] NASA Federal Acquisition Regulation Supplement (NFS) § 1843.7005(a).

The NFS allows for such use of UCAs on an exception basis and also notes that, when UCAs are used, the agency's liabilities and commitments must be minimized.[29] As figure 4 illustrates, the booster and main engine element contractors performed development work under UCAs for more than a year and the core stage and ICPS contractor continued those elements' development under UCAs for 2 years or more.

Figure 4: Months Each SLS Element Spent under Undefinitized Contract Actions

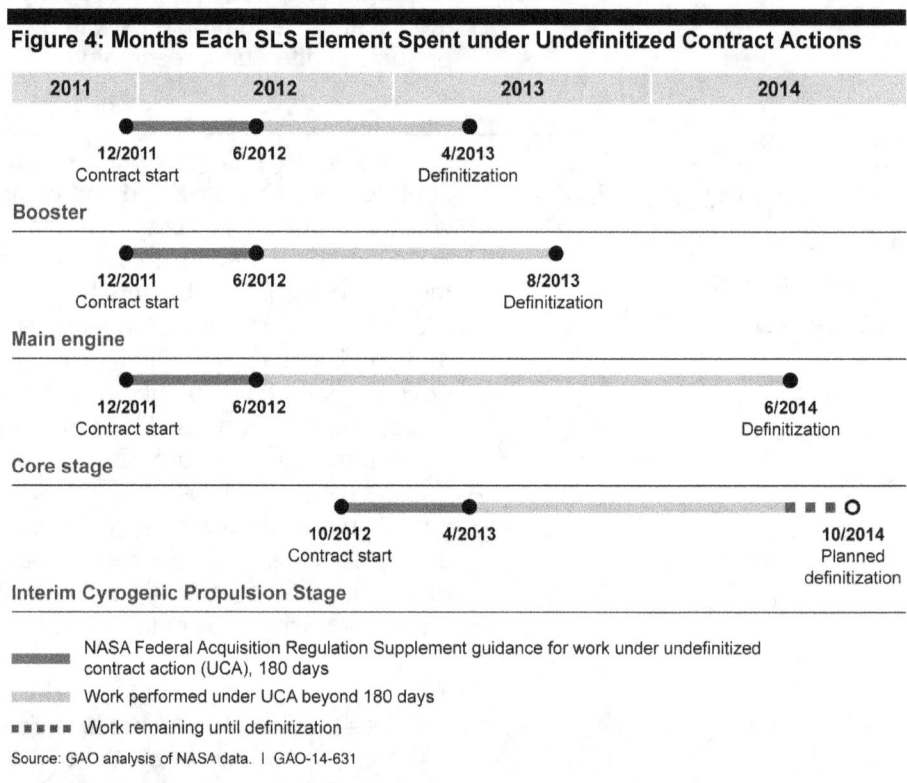

Source: GAO analysis of NASA data. | GAO-14-631

NASA allowed high-value modifications to the SLS contracts to remain undefinitized for extended periods—in one instance a contract remained undefinitized for 30 months. Because lack of agreement on contract terms prolonged NASA's timeframes for finalizing SLS contracts, the establishment of contractor cost and schedule baselines necessary to monitor performance was delayed. Specifically, in most cases, the SLS program did not receive complete earned value management (EVM) data

---

[29] NFS § 1843.7002(a).

derived from approved baselines on these SLS contracts. Earned value, or the planned cost of completed work and work in progress, can provide accurate assessments of project progress, produce early warning signs of impending schedule delays and cost overruns, and provide unbiased estimates of anticipated costs at completion. The use of EVM, which integrates the project scope of work with cost, schedule, and performance elements for optimum project planning and control, is advocated by both GAO's best practices for cost estimating and NASA's own guidance.[30] Without having a contracted baseline against which to measure the earned value, the program is missing a useful indicator of true program status—in the case of SLS, the program's performance toward its 2017 launch date.

The program began receiving EVM data from the booster contractor in 2013, and began receiving it from the main engine contractor in 2014, but has yet to receive EVM data from the core stage or ICPS contractors because, according to program officials, the core stage contract was just definitized and the ICPS contract has yet to be definitized and baselines have yet to be established. We have previously found that UCAs transfer cost and performance risk from the contractor to the government.[31] Our earned value body of work indicates that an integrated baseline review can help allay that risk by providing the government with assurance that the performance baseline reflects all requirements and that resources are adequate to complete the work.[32] Program officials stated that they planned to hold an integrated baseline review for each element, following contract definitization, in order to begin receiving EVM data from the element contractors. In lieu of EVM, according to program officials, the contractors have been providing cost and schedule data to NASA derived

---

[30] GAO-09-3SP and NPR 7120.5E, § 2.2.8 (Aug. 14, 2012).

[31] GAO, *Defense Contract Management: DOD's Lack of Adherence to Key Contracting Principles on Iraq Oil Contract Put Government Interests at Risk*, GAO-07-839 (Washington, D.C.: Jul. 31, 2007); *Defense Contracting: Use of Undefinitized Contract Actions Understated and Definitization Time Frames Often Not Met*, GAO-07-559 (Washington, D.C.: Jun. 19, 2007); and *Rebuilding Iraq: Fiscal Year 2003 Contract Award Procedures and Management Challenges*, GAO-04-605 (Washington, D.C.: Jun. 1, 2004).

[32] See, for example, GAO, *NASA: Earned Value Management Implementation across Major Spaceflight Projects Is Uneven*, GAO-13-22, (Washington, D.C.: Nov. 19, 2012); *Defense Acquisitions: Missile Defense Program Instability Affects Reliability of Earned Value Management Data*, GAO-10-676 (Washington, D.C.: Jul. 14, 2010); and GAO-09-3SP.

from their internal baselines. Until the program and the contractor reach final agreement on contract terms, however, this data may not reflect whether the contractor is accomplishing the work planned within the agency's allocated cost and schedule. Until baselines are set and an integrated baseline review is held, the cost and schedule data can only be used as indicators of progress. Furthermore, such data can be misleading as it lacks a comparison between work performed versus planned.

SLS Program Has Critical Gaps in Knowledge Needed to Assess Long-Term Affordability, but Opportunities Exist to Promote Affordability

NASA has yet to make mission decisions beyond EM-2 for the SLS program and has not produced a complete life-cycle cost estimate for any of the three planned variants; however, competition opportunities exist for future development work that may promote long-term affordability. Although the agency has identified several possible destinations, it has not decided upon specific missions for the SLS program beyond EM-1 and EM-2, which will directly affect the program's future development path and flight schedule. Mission selection will likely determine the order of future development efforts, as the program can only afford to develop one upgraded element at a time. Each development effort may be large enough to constitute a separate project, but the full magnitude of these development efforts is unknown as the program has not established cost estimates for any of the three SLS variants, including the 70-mt vehicle, beyond 2017. Although the program costs are as yet unknown, there are opportunities to improve long-term affordability through competition once the element upgrade development path has been determined. While the main engine contractor for future SLS vehicles is likely to remain the same, the program plans to compete the acquisition of the advanced boosters. Additionally, the program could compete the acquisition of several other elements in order to potentially reduce costs.

The SLS Program's Long-Term Mission Plans and Requirements Are Unknown

NASA has not yet defined specific mission requirements for any variant of the SLS. The two currently scheduled flights, EM-1 and EM-2, are developmental test flights designed to demonstrate and test the capabilities of the 70-mt launch vehicle and the capability of the core stage in particular. Office of Management and Budget guidance indicates that agencies should develop long range objectives, supported by detailed budgets and plans that identify the agency's performance gaps and the resources needed to close them.[33] According to agency officials, beyond the two scheduled test flights, no future mission destinations have been determined. In the absence of specific mission requirements, officials indicated the SLS program is developing the variants based on top-level requirements derived from NASA's Design Reference Architectures that lay out the technical and scientific framework for conducting missions in line with the agency's strategic plan. NASA's 2014 strategic plan, for example, identifies sending humans to Mars as one of the agency's long-term goals; in turn, the agency's Mars Design Reference Architecture indicates that multiple missions using a vehicle with a lift capability of about 130 mt will be necessary to support that goal.

Although NASA is considering long-term Mars missions and asteroid redirect missions, NASA has not yet finalized plans for the next step in evolving the SLS and risks investing limited available resources in systems and designs that are not yet needed. The agency intends to use the same core stage design for all variants of the SLS, but it will be faced with replacing all the other major hardware elements used on the 70-mt vehicle—that is, the upper stage, boosters, and engines—so that the 105- and 130-mt vehicles can perform missions that support the agency's strategic goals of carrying heavier payloads and traveling deeper into space. To that end, NASA is working on analyses and concept designs for a new upper stage and for advanced boosters. Because mission requirements for the 105-mt variant are not yet defined, however, NASA faces the possibility that it will spend time and money developing systems and designs that may not be needed for the specific mission that will be defined. For example, according to program officials and as illustrated in figure 5, in order to have a 105-mt capability ready to launch soon after 2021, the agency must make a decision not later than 2016 about whether it will first pursue development of the upper stage or advanced boosters as the next step in increasing SLS capability beyond the 70-mt variant.

---

[33] Office of Management and Budget, *OMB Circular A-11, Supplement for Part 7: Capital Programming Guide* (Washington, D.C.: July 2013).

Figure 5: SLS 2016 Vehicle Development Decision

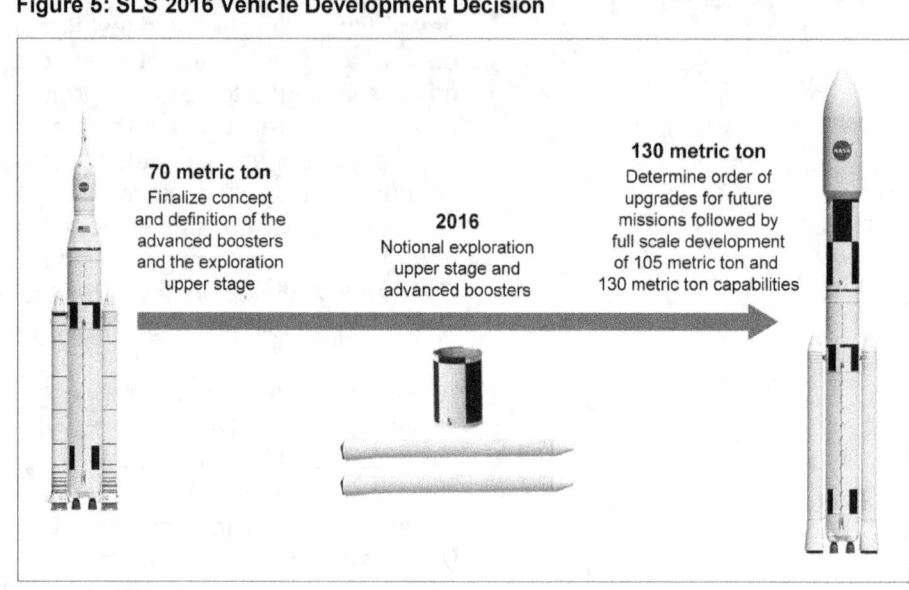

70 metric ton
Finalize concept
and definition of the
advanced boosters
and the exploration
upper stage

2016
Notional exploration
upper stage and
advanced boosters

130 metric ton
Determine order of
upgrades for future
missions followed by
full scale development
of 105 metric ton and
130 metric ton capabilities

Source: GAO presentation of NASA data. | GAO-14-631

Program officials stated that the agency does not have resources to conduct more than one development effort at a time and that it is difficult to determine which system to develop first because each improves SLS lift capability in different ways. A new upper stage would provide more capability beyond Earth orbit and better support missions that require more in-space propulsion, such as missions to a near-Earth asteroid or other distant locations. Advanced boosters would provide more capability to low-Earth orbit and better support missions that require the SLS to place a larger payload in orbit around the Earth. No matter which effort NASA pursues, in order for the agency to begin full-scale development after 2016, it is confronted with requesting related funding in the year before it plans to begin work. For example, if NASA intends to initiate full-scale upper stage development in 2017, including the related funding request in its fiscal year 2016 budget submission would be prudent. The sooner NASA makes a decision about which development to pursue first, the sooner it will be able to focus its limited resources on the chosen effort. Conversely, the longer the agency delays the decision, the more likely it will expend those resources on a design that might not yet be needed.

Regardless of when the mission requirements are established and what development NASA first pursues, those future development efforts are likely to be of sufficient cost and scope to constitute programs or projects in and of themselves. According to NASA officials, the advanced booster and new upper stage, for example, will involve distinct development, integration, qualification, and testing efforts. As such, they meet NASA's own criteria for a new project in that they will represent a specific effort with defined requirements, a life-cycle cost estimate, and a beginning and end, and will result in new or revised products, in the form of improved boosters and stages, to address strategic goals. Further, these efforts are likely to far exceed the $250 million life-cycle cost established in NASA policy as the threshold for requiring the NASA Associate Administrator approval of cost and schedule baseline commitments.[34] These projects are subject to oversight by senior agency officials through periodic programmatic reviews that assess technical and programmatic readiness to move forward at various decision points. At this time, future SLS development efforts are not planned to be managed as separate projects, though NASA has indicated that it plans to hold design reviews for these efforts consistent with its acquisition policies and practices. Best practices for system acquisition and cost estimating advocate an evolutionary approach wherein each capability increment has its own cost, schedule, and performance baselines and methods to report progress against these baselines.[35] In addition, we have previously concluded that it is prudent for an agency to manage increasing capabilities of an existing program on par with the level of investments yet to come and in a way that is beneficial for oversight. For example, we have recommended that agencies developing weapon systems in increments consider establishing each increment of increased capability with its own cost and schedule baseline.[36] Establishing cost, schedule, and performance baselines for each increment that has costs exceeding $250 million could provide decision makers with additional insights into the progress and long-term affordability of each increment.

---

[34] NPR 7120.5 E (Aug. 14, 2012).

[35] GAO-09-3SP; GAO-04-386SP; and GAO-01-288.

[36] GAO, *Tactical Aircraft: F-22A Modernization Program Faces Cost, Technical, and Sustainment Risks*, GAO-12-447 (Washington D.C.: May 2, 2012).

The Program's Long-Term Affordability Is Unknown Because SLS Cost Estimate Does Not Capture Life Cycle Costs

The long-term affordability of the SLS program is also unknown, as we found in May 2014, because NASA's baseline cost estimate for the program will not provide any information about the longer-term, life cycle costs of developing, manufacturing, and operating the launch vehicle.[37] NASA does not plan for that baseline estimate, which will be established when SLS moves into implementation, to cover program costs after EM-1 or costs to design, develop, build, and produce the 105- or 130-mt variants.

Based on the tenets of widely-accepted best practices for cost estimation as well as NASA's own requirements and guidance regarding life cycle costs, in May 2014 we made recommendations to enhance transparency, assist congressional oversight, and ensure insight into affordability as the agency moves ahead with the SLS, Orion, and related ground support programs.[38] In terms of SLS, we recommended that NASA establish a separate cost and schedule baseline for work required to support SLS Block I EM-2 and report that information via its annual budget submission. As part of that recommendation, we noted that, if NASA decides to fly the SLS Block I 70-mt variant beyond EM-2, the agency should then establish separate life cycle cost and schedule baseline estimates for that variant and report this information via its annual budget submission. Additionally, we recommended that NASA establish life cycle cost and schedule baselines for each upgraded block of the SLS, Orion, and associated ground support. We stated that, if the agency believed it could not do so because missions and flight manifests were unknown, then it should forecast minimum and maximum ranges for the increased capabilities' life cycle costs in its annual budget submission. NASA partially concurred with our recommendations, citing among other reasons that actions already in place such as establishing SLS, Orion, and related ground support as separate programs and a block upgrade approach for SLS— and actions it plans to take to track costs—met the intent of our recommendations.

---

[37] GAO, *NASA: Actions Needed to Improve Transparency and Assess Long-Term Affordability of Human Exploration Programs*, GAO-14-385, (Washington D.C.: May 8, 2014).

[38] GAO-09-3SP; NPR 7120.5E § 2.4(Aug. 14, 2012); *2008 NASA Cost Estimating Handbook; and* GAO-14-385.

In our evaluation of NASA's comments, we acknowledged that these actions were a step in the right direction, but noted that NASA's actions do not fully address our concerns. Specifically, we pointed out that establishing cost and schedule at the broader program level was unlikely to provide the detail necessary to monitor the progress of each block against a baseline; it was unclear from NASA's response whether cost commitments the agency plans within the SLS design review process would serve the same purpose as establishing a cost baseline for each respective upgrade; and reporting costs associated with EM-2 and subsequent variants of SLS via the agency's annual budget submission would not provide information about potential costs over the long term because budget requests neither offer all the same information as life-cycle cost estimates nor are necessarily linked to an established baseline that indicates how much NASA expects to invest to develop, operate, and sustain a capability over the long-term. We stated that, as NASA establishes parameters for the additional flights of the first SLS capability and upgraded capabilities, including flight rates, mission destinations, and other requirements, it will be well-poised to move from reporting costs in budget submissions to establishing baseline cost and schedule estimates for each capability and reporting progress against these respective baselines.

NASA Taking Steps for Long-Term Affordability but Additional Opportunities May Exist

NASA has taken some steps that may promote the long-term affordability of the SLS program as directed in the National Space Transportation Policy.[39] The policy requires that human space flight development efforts such as the SLS program identify and implement measures to enhance affordability. To promote affordability, SLS has funded a series of studies and assessments on advanced boosters by both potential industry partners and universities. According to program officials, these activities—which include improved welding procedures, simulation of material performance, and demonstration of potential propellants—may provide better understanding of the processes, structures, and risk levels of various booster development options, which may in turn reduce the cost or schedule necessary to design and develop an advanced booster. Program officials also indicated that such activities may provide better insight into which contractors may compete for future booster development contracts.

---

[39] National Space Transportation Policy. (Nov. 21, 2013).

The program, however, could promote longer term affordability by introducing competition in the development and production contracts for other hardware elements. Our body of work on contracting has shown that competition in contracting is a key element for maintaining cost control.[40] We have found that promoting competition increases the potential for acquiring quality goods and services at a lower price and that noncompetitive contracts carry the risk of overspending because, among other reasons, they have been negotiated without the benefit of competition to help establish pricing. NASA has structured other launch programs, such as the Commercial Crew and Launch Services Program, based on the premise that competition will lower costs. In addition, the NASA Authorization Act of 2010 requires that NASA compete sub-elements of the SLS. Furthermore, with certain exceptions, full and open competition in soliciting offers and awarding contracts is generally a requirement of the Competition in Contracting Act of 1984 and the Federal Acquisition Regulation.[41] Given the long-term planned use of SLS, using non-competitive procedures to acquire any portion of the SLS vehicle may lead to higher costs that could be felt for years or decades.

As it replaces hardware elements used on the 70-mt variant with elements necessary to support NASA's anticipated uses of the 105- and 130-mt variants, the SLS program will likely have several opportunities to promote long-term affordability through competing contracts for the new elements. The program plans to use only the core stage and main engines for all flights beyond EM-2. Program briefings indicate that the SLS program optimized the design of the core stage, which will be used with all vehicle variants, to utilize the RS-25 engines remaining from the Space Shuttle program. According to agency officials, a natural consequence of finalizing the core stage design based on the RS-25 is that the only engine-related efforts open to future competition will be RS-25 subsystems and components. The program could be in a favorable position, however, to compete contracts for the exploration upper stage,

---

[40] See, for example, GAO, *Federal Contracting: Noncompetitive Contracts Based on Urgency Need Additional Oversight*, GAO-14-304 (Washington, D.C.: Mar. 26, 2014); *Defense Contracting: Actions Needed to Increase Competition*, GAO-13-325 (Washington, D.C.: Mar. 28, 2013); and *Federal Contracting: Opportunities Exist to Increase Competition and Assess Reasons When Only One Offer Is Received*, GAO-10-833 (Washington, D.C.: Jul. 26, 2010).

[41] Pub. L. No. 98-369, § 2711, 98 Stat. 494, 1175; and Federal Acquisition Regulation § 6.101(a).

the upper stage engine, and advanced boosters that it expects to use on the 105- and 130-mt variants. According to SLS program officials, it currently plans to compete contracts for the development and production of new advanced boosters that will be more capable than the current five-segment boosters. The program is considering multiple design solutions including metallic or composite casings and liquid or solid fuel. Based on our review of program documentation and discussions with agency officials, however, additional opportunities exist to compete the procurement of other sub-elements needed for the 105- and 130-mt vehicles. In some cases other programs, both within and outside of NASA, use alternative hardware that serves similar purposes.

- According to program officials, the program plans to procure a new upper stage through the existing core stage contract to replace the ICPS, which the program is using as an interim solution, for all missions following EM-2. They also stated that the program does not plan to compete the upper stage development because its initial award to Boeing in 2007 under the Constellation program was done competitively. Since that award, however, our work indicates that the marketplace for spacecraft development has shifted considerably as new commercial providers have since developed and have launched, or are currently developing, upper stages. These providers may offer viable competition for the new upper stage. For example, in recent years Orbital Sciences Corporation and SpaceX have successfully flown upper stages for NASA's Commercial Cargo program and SpaceX and Boeing will need to human-rate upper stages as part of NASA's Commercial Crew program with flights expected to begin around 2017.

- The SLS program must also procure a new upper stage engine. According to NASA officials, the upper stage engine will be selected based on mission need. Potential competitors include Aerojet Rocketdyne's J-2X, the Evolved Expandable Launch Vehicle's RL10, and the BE-3 engine that Blue Origin is developing for the Commercial Crew program, among other options.

Because, except for the RS-25 engines, NASA's current contracting approach for the SLS program, does not commit the program beyond the hardware needed for EM-2, moving forward the agency will be in the position to take advantage of the evolving launch vehicle market. An updated assessment of the launch vehicle market could better position NASA to sustain competition, control costs, and better inform the Congress about the long-term affordability of the program.

Conclusions

NASA established the SLS program to provide the capability for transporting humans into space, but the agency is unlikely to do so as quickly as it intended. The initial launch date for SLS is just 3 and a half years away. That is a short time given the amount of development, integration, and testing that must occur for the vehicle to fly in 2017. While the technical challenges associated with those efforts appear manageable, the compressed development schedule in conjunction with the agency's relatively flat funding profile for SLS through 2017 place the program at high risk of missing the planned December 2017 launch date for the EM-1 initial test flight.

Beyond the SLS second flight in 2021, the program's path is unclear. NASA is waiting for additional policy direction on future missions, but the agency is approaching a crossroads wherein it is confronted with defining a developmental path forward to the more capable variants of SLS. Without identifying a range of mission possibilities and their required funding, the program is at risk of making uninformed decisions and pursuing development paths that may not make the most efficient use of limited resources in the near term and could negatively impact longer term affordability. Furthermore, without this information the agency's ability to make important decisions about the affordability of the program in the context of the agency's overall budget and competing priorities is limited. Additionally, it is unclear how the agency plans to manage the upgraded capability efforts. Without carefully structuring the approach for future variants, decision makers will lack transparency into costs and will be limited in their ability to assess long-term affordability and progress. This lack of knowledge about program direction and cost is of concern because the success of these programs will be measured by both the capabilities they achieve and their affordability. NASA has at its disposal one critical tool for addressing SLS affordability concerns—competition—more specifically, competition for procurement associated with the two variants' elements. While NASA is planning to compete procurement of the advanced boosters, the agency also has opportunities to compete procurement of other upgraded elements, including the upper stage and the upper stage engine to help it achieve long-term affordability.

Recommendations for Executive Action

To provide the Congress with the necessary insight into program planning and affordability, and to decrease the risk of cost and schedule overruns, we recommend that NASA's Administrator direct the Human Exploration and Operations Mission Directorate to take the following four actions:

- NASA should develop an executable business case for SLS based on matching requirements and resources that results in a level of risk commensurate with its policies. For example, NASA could delay the planned first flight test or increase funding to allow the program to establish cost and schedule baselines for demonstration of the initial capability at the 70 percent confidence level.

- To provide decision makers with an informed basis for making investment decisions regarding the SLS program, NASA should identify a range of possible missions for each future SLS variant that includes cost and schedule estimates and plans for how those possible missions would fit within NASA's funding profile.

- To allow for a continued assessment of progress and affordability, NASA should structure each future increment of SLS capability with a total cost exceeding the $250 million threshold for designation as a major project as a separate development effort within the SLS program. In doing so, NASA should require each increment to complete both the technical and programmatic reviews required of other major development projects, per the agency's acquisition and system engineering policies.

- To promote affordability, before finalizing acquisition plans for future capability variants, NASA should assess the full range of competition opportunities and provide to the Congress the agency's assessment of the extent to which development and production of future elements of the SLS could be competitively procured.

Agency Comments

NASA provided written comments on a draft of this report. These comments are reprinted in appendix II.

In written and oral comments on a draft of this report, NASA concurred with our four recommendations. NASA agreed that future increments of SLS should be structured as separate development efforts and indicated that those increments would be subject to the appropriate technical and programmatic reviews, as well as rigorous cost and schedule management. NASA also recognized the need to define missions to guide program planning and indicated it will develop plans for specific SLS missions within NASA's standard mission selection and review process.

We would expect that this process would also include cost and schedule estimates associated with each option and plans for how these possible missions would fit within NASA's funding profile. NASA acknowledged the importance of establishing a business case and cost and schedule baselines for the SLS program consistent with NASA policies and recognized that the program's schedule may have to be revised to accommodate decreased funding levels or to address technical problems. We would expect that an executable business case for the SLS program would be based on cost and schedule baselines that reflect a joint cost and schedule confidence level of 70 percent. NASA also indicated it would assess opportunities for increased competition and follow all applicable federal and NASA acquisition regulations governing competition within its contracting activities. As our recommendation indicates, NASA's assessment of competitive procurement opportunities should address development and production of all future elements of the SLS, including the upper stage, and result in a report of this current assessment to the Congress. Separately, NASA provided technical comments, which have been incorporated into the report, as appropriate.

We are sending this report to NASA's Administrator and to interested congressional committees. In addition, the report will be available at no charge on GAO's website at http://www.gao.gov.

Should you or your staff have any questions on matters discussed in this report, please contact me at (202) 512-4841 or chaplainc@gao.gov. Contact points for our Offices of Congressional Relations and Public Affairs may be found on the last page of this report. Other key contributors to this report are listed in appendix III.

Sincerely yours,

Cristina T. Chaplain
Director
Acquisition and Sourcing Management

Appendix I: Scope and Methodology

In order to assess the National Aeronautics and Space Administration's (NASA) progress to conduct its first flight in 2017, we interviewed and obtained briefings and relevant documents from NASA and contractor officials. We identified and evaluated technical and programmatic issues associated with each major Space Launch System (SLS) element, including new and heritage hardware, by reviewing associated development plans and discussing relevant schedules and issues with agency officials. We also compared planned and actual progress in maturing system designs at the element and program level and evaluated how delays in element maturation and integration could affect the SLS program as a whole. We assessed NASA's risk mitigation plans for SLS to gauge the program's progress in addressing technical issues and to evaluate the potential cost and schedule impact to program milestones, including events such as delivery and flight dates. We also reviewed other technical and programmatic indicators—including progress against mass and performance goals, progress made addressing required actions from programmatic reviews at both the subsystem and vehicle level, and the status of schedule threats to the program's critical path—and assessed program status against those indicators. We assessed the status of the program's allocation of top level requirements to the different elements and the preparation of verification and validation plans for those requirements at the preliminary design review. We also evaluated the status of contracting activities for each element, including determining whether respective contracts were definitized and baselined and whether earned value information about contractor progress against planned cost and schedule was available to the program.

To assess long-term affordability, we discussed long-term development plans in support of future missions with agency officials. We also reviewed the design reference architecture establishing the need for the large launch vehicle and compared the program's approach for satisfying the need to the agency's strategic plan. For purposes of assessing the cost estimate, we reviewed NASA preliminary cost estimates for the SLS, Orion, and associated ground systems programs and information related to NASA's plans for the SLS baseline cost estimate in order to determine the scope of the estimates and assessed whether that scope provided transparency into costs and enabled assessment of long-term affordability. We assessed the preliminary estimates' scope against best practices criteria outlined in GAO's cost estimating guidebook as well as NASA's own guidance and procedural requirements. We also discussed the estimate with NASA officials, including the rationale for the estimates' scope and exclusions to that scope. As NASA had not released the baseline estimate for SLS at the time of our review, we did not asses the reliability of the SLS baseline estimate. Furthermore, we evaluated the program's development and acquisition plans to compete future variants of the SLS by reviewing contract information, including any follow-on contract options, and discussing supplier availability with agency officials.

We conducted our work at locations where the SLS program is being managed and executed including NASA headquarters in Washington, D.C.; NASA's Kennedy Space Flight Center in Cape Canaveral, Fla.; NASA's Marshall Space Flight Center in Huntsville, Ala.; AeroJet Rocketdyne in Canoga Park, Calif.; Alliant Technologies in Promontory, Utah; and the Boeing Company in Huntsville, Ala.

We conducted this performance audit from June 2013 to July 2014 in accordance with generally accepted government auditing standards. Those standards require that we plan and perform the audit to obtain sufficient, appropriate evidence to provide a reasonable basis for our findings and conclusions based on our audit objectives. We believe that the evidence obtained provides a reasonable basis for our findings and conclusions based on our audit objectives.

Appendix II: Comments from the National Aeronautics and Space Administration

National Aeronautics and Space Administration

Office of the Administrator
Washington, DC 20546-0001

JUL 1 4 2014

Human Exploration and Operations Mission Directorate

Cristina T. Chaplain
Director
Acquisition Sourcing Management
United States Government Accountability Office
Washington, DC 20548

Dear Mrs. Chaplain:

The National Aeronautics and Space Administration (NASA) appreciates the opportunity to review and comment on the Government Accountability Office (GAO) draft report entitled, "Space Launch System: Business Case Needed to Decrease Risk and Support Long Term Affordability" (GAO-14-631). In order to properly respond to the GAO recommendations, NASA believes it is important to put this report on SLS in the broader context of the Agency's overall exploration strategy.

NASA appreciates GAO's recognition of the significant progress that SLS has made since the program entered pre-formulation in 2011. As GAO noted, SLS has remained on track to an aggressive schedule for launch readiness in December 2017. Requirements have been defined and verified, design drawings are being delivered on or ahead of schedule, mass and performance margins are being maintained, prototype hardware is being manufactured, tests are on track, and the program is on plan for critical design review in 2015. The GAO noted areas where there continue to be some technical challenges, which is to be expected in a development project on the scale of SLS, but none were considered to be significant given proper program vigilance. GAO highlighted the status of contract definitization and implications for understanding the full program risk posture, particularly in terms of having baselined earned value management data from the contractors. The GAO did not identify any specific issues that were not already being worked by the program, which reflects NASA's detailed and continuous oversight of contractor work during the undefinitized contract period. Three of the four prime contracts (for Core Stage, Engines, and Boosters) have been definitized, and the fourth (for the Interim Cryogenic Propulsion Stage) is on track for definitization this fall.

As the GAO notes, SLS (along with the Orion Multi-Purpose Crew Vehicle and the Ground Systems Development and Operations programs) are being designed as foundational capabilities for human exploration in deep-space. The capability-based architecture is designed for long-term human exploration of our inner solar system, with a horizon goal of landing humans on Mars. Both SLS and Orion are being designed to

2

enable multiple exploration missions and destinations rather than being optimized for one particular exploration mission or architecture.

This is a critical point, one that is at the core of a NASA capability-driven exploration strategy that traces back to the NASA Authorization Act of 2010. NASA has developed an exploration concept of operations that defines both the required tactical (near-term, in the proving ground of trans-lunar space) and strategic (long-term, in preparation for exploration missions to Mars) capabilities for SLS. These requirements are being refined in the context of an evolvable Mars campaign concept that builds upon the initial concept of operations and Level I requirements. The evolvable Mars campaign will be developed to maximize learning opportunities, provide flexibility to adjust based upon what is learned through exploration activities in the proving ground of cis-lunar space, and progress in accordance with the national budget environment. In essence, through this flexible, capability-driven framework, NASA applies the lessons of knowledge-based decision making to the exploration architecture as a whole.

As the GAO acknowledges, the evolvable nature of SLS is consistent with procurement best-practices for buying down program risk; likewise, evolvability in the service of affordability is also a key component of the capability-driven architecture. SLS is designed for the express purpose of enabling multi-decade human exploration beyond low-Earth orbit in support of national objectives and policy. The requirements for a safe and reliable human exploration transportation system (particularly in terms of lift capacity and volume) are significantly greater than for non-exploration missions. As an example of the SLS capabilities, the Block 1 SLS will have over two and a half times – and Block 2 over four times – the lift capacity to low Earth orbit compared with existing launch vehicles. The capabilities of SLS are even more pronounced for missions beyond low Earth orbit, where SLS is intended to deliver from two to over eight times the payload mass to Mars, in a single launch, and beyond compared to existing vehicles.

Taken together, the capability-based framework and the evolvable architecture for SLS provide the foundation for a knowledge-based approach to exploration. From this strategy, NASA has identified conceptual missions that provide defined minimum capabilities for SLS (such as required mass delivered to lunar or Martian orbit), while the basic timing of those missions (operating in trans-lunar space through the 2020s, with Mars missions in the 2030s) drives when upgraded SLS capabilities are required.

Accordingly, this evolvable Mars concept does not readily lend itself to classical life cycle definitions. NASA acknowledges that it does not yet know how many launches of what version of SLS will be required for the first Mars mission, or what exact series of intermediate missions (ones that will have their own intrinsic worth beyond their value as precursors to Mars) will be the stepping stones on the way to Mars. Further, SLS may have uses beyond human exploration of the inner solar system. Within this framework, two facts are beyond dispute. One, in order to maximize the chances of success for missions to deep space (and certainly missions to Mars), a launch vehicle with the lift and in-space performance envisioned for SLS is required. Two, if missions to deep space and ultimately Mars are to be affordable, it is vital to minimize the costs to develop, operate,

3

and upgrade SLS. It is in the context of this latter point, in particular, that NASA appreciates the work of GAO in providing their recommendations.

In the draft report, GAO recommends that the NASA Administrator direct the Human Exploration and Operations Mission Directorate take the following actions:

Recommendation 1: NASA should develop an executable business case for SLS based on matching requirements and resources that results in a level of risk commensurate with its policies. For example, NASA could delay the planned first flight test or increase funding to allow the program to establish cost and schedule baselines for demonstration of the initial capability at the 70 percent confidence level.

Management's Response: NASA understands the recommendation and concurs with the intent. The agency baseline cost and schedule commitment for SLS will be made consistent with NASA policy and documented in the SLS Key Decision Point C Decision Memorandum. NASA has and will continue to properly balance risk within SLS and across the exploration portfolio. An important (and widely used) element of managing risks is to manage a program to a schedule that provides margin against the agency commitment, to protect against schedule threats that may arise during development. Consistent with the discussion above, with SLS NASA is developing a capability that is affordable and sustainable over the long term. In this context, delaying the SLS development schedule or diverting funding from other priorities to satisfy a schedule confidence level could jeopardize these goals and result in an increase in costs to the taxpayer. Plans are in place to adjust schedule and minimize costs within the agency commitment if either funding levels decrease or technical problems arise.

Recommendation 2: To provide decision makers with an informed basis for making investment decisions regarding the SLS program, NASA should identify a range of possible missions for each future SLS variant that includes cost and schedule estimates and plans for how those possible missions would fit within NASA's funding profile.

Management Response: NASA concurs with the recommendation. NASA has documented tactical (near-term) and strategic (in preparation for Mars) capabilities for SLS. Planning for specific missions will follow standard applicable NASA mission selection and review processes for ongoing operations.

Recommendation 3: To allow for a continued assessment of progress and affordability, NASA should structure each future increment of SLS capability with a total cost exceeding the $250 million threshold for designation as a separate development effort within the SLS program. In doing so, NASA should require each increment to complete both the technical and programmatic reviews required of other major development projects, per the agency's acquisition and system engineering policies.

Management Response: NASA concurs with the recommendation. For major block element upgrades (specifically the Exploration Upper Stage and Advanced Boosters),

4

NASA will conduct appropriate element and vehicle-level technical design and programmatic reviews and perform rigorous cost and schedule management of the development of these elements in the context of overall SLS program goals.

Recommendation 4: To promote affordability, before finalizing acquisition plans for future capability variants, NASA should assess the full range of competition opportunities and provide to the Congress the agency's assessment of the extent to which development and production of future elements of the SLS could be competitively procured.

Management Response: NASA concurs with the recommendation. NASA will follow all applicable federal and NASA supplemental acquisition regulations, including full justification on any proposed contract action for other than full and open competition.

Thank you for the opportunity to comment on this draft report. If you have any questions or require additional information, please contact Michelle Bascoe at (202) 358-1574.

Sincerely,

William Gerstenmaier
Associate Administrator
for Human Exploration and Operations

Appendix III: GAO Contact and Staff Acknowledgments

GAO Contact

Cristina T. Chaplain (202) 512-4841 or chaplainc@gao.gov.

Staff Acknowledgments

In addition to the contact named above, Shelby S. Oakley (Assistant Director), Andrea M. Bivens, Tana M. Davis, Laura Greifner, Sylvia Schatz, Ryan Stott, Roxanna T. Sun, and John S. Warren, Jr. made key contributions to this report.